D0931563

LITTLE BIOGRAPHIES OF BIG PEOPLE

MELANIA TRUMP

By Joan Stoltman

Gareth Stevens
PUBLISHING

Please visit our website, www.garethstevens.com. For a free color catalog of all our high-quality books, call toll free 1-800-542-2595 or fax 1-877-542-2596.

Library of Congress Cataloging-in-Publication Data

Names: Stoltman, Joan, author.
Title: Melania Trump / Joan Stoltman.
Description: New York : Gareth Stevens Publishing, 2019. | Series: Little
    biographies of big people | Includes index.
Identifiers: LCCN 2018023552| ISBN 9781538228968 (library bound) | ISBN
    9781538231661 (pbk.) | ISBN 9781538232231 (6 pack)
Subjects: LCSH: Trump, Melania, 1970—Juvenile literature. | Presidents'
    spouses–United States–Biography–Juvenile literature.
Classification: LCC E914.T77 S76 2019 | DDC 973.933092 [B] –dc23
LC record available at https://lccn.loc.gov/2018023552

Published in 2019 by
Gareth Stevens Publishing
111 East 14th Street, Suite 349
New York, NY 10003

Designer: Tanya Dellaccio
Editor: Kate Mikoley

Photo credits: series art Yulia Glam/Shutterstock.com; cover, p. 1 Monica Schipper/
FilmMagic/Getty Images; p. 5 Chip Somodevilla/Getty Images News/Getty Images;
p. 7 CAPEHART/Getty Images Entertainment/Getty Images; p. 9 NG HAN GUAN/AFP/
Getty Images; p. 11 Scott Gries/Hulton Archive/Getty Images; p. 13 NurPhoto/Getty
Images; p. 15 BRENDAN SMIALOWSKI/AFP/Getty Images; pp. 17, 21 JIM WATSON/
AFP/Getty Images; p. 19 Bloomberg/Getty Images.

Printed in the United States of America

CPSIA compliance information: Batch #CW19GS: For further information contact Gareth Stevens, New York, New York at 1-800-542-2595.

CONTENTS

Boldface words appear in the glossary.

Far Away

Melania Trump was born Melanija Knavs in 1970 in Yugoslavia. At the time, Yugoslavia was a **Communist** country. Later, it became many smaller countries. The part Melania is from is now called Slovenia. Her father was a businessman who sold cars.

5

Loving Fashion Early

Melania's mother worked at a clothing factory for more than 30 years. After work, she'd often sew clothes for Melania and her sister, Ines. Melania loved to read the fashion **magazines** her mother brought back from work trips.

INES KNAUSS

Melania began drawing clothing **designs** for her mother and sister to sew. She even made her own **jewelry**! In 1985, Melania went to a design high school. After finishing there, she started at a **college** to study design.

Becoming a Model

When Melania was 16, a fashion **photographer** saw her and suggested she become a **model**. A few years later, she left Slovenia for modeling jobs. Melania has worked with some of the best fashion photographers and fashion magazines in the world!

11

Off to the United States

In 1996, Melania moved to New York for modeling work. Soon, she met Donald Trump. In 2005, Melania and Donald married. In 2006, Melania became a US citizen. The same year, Melania and Donald's son, Barron, was born.

BARRON TRUMP

13

A Mother First

Melania has spent time helping others through her work with groups such as the American Red Cross. She's also worked on her own jewelry line. However, she's said her most important job is being a mom. She tries to do most of her work when Barron is at school.

15

First Lady

In 2017, Melania became First Lady when Donald became president of the United States. She's the only First Lady to not speak English as her first language. She's also only the second First Lady to be born in another country.

PRESIDENT DONALD TRUMP

First Ladies often take on a cause while they're in the White House. Melania chose to work on helping children and stopping cyberbullying. Cyberbullying is when people are mean to each other online, or through cell phones or computers.

"The well-being of children is of the **utmost** importance to me and I plan to use my **platform** as First Lady to help as many kids as I can."
—Melania Trump

Believe

Even as a child, Melania had confidence, or the feeling that she could do well and succeed. When she became First Lady, she became known around the world. But even before that, she worked hard to follow her dreams!

GLOSSARY

college: a school after high school

Communist: a kind of government in which there is no private property and the government owns the things that are used to make and move products such as land, oil, and factories

design: the pattern or shape of something. Also, to create the pattern or shape of something.

jewelry: decorative objects (such as rings, necklaces, and earrings) that people wear on their body

magazine: a type of thin book with a paper cover that contains stories and pictures and is usually printed every week or month

model: a person whose job it is to show clothes or other things for sale by wearing or using them

photographer: a person who takes pictures with a camera especially as a job

platform: something that allows someone to tell a large number of people about an idea

utmost: greatest or highest in amount

FOR MORE INFORMATION

BOOKS

Krull, Kathleen. *A Kids' Guide to America's First Ladies.* New York, NY: HarperCollins, 2017.

Oachs, Emily Rose. *Melania Trump: Champion for Youth.* Mankato, MN: Child's World, 2018.

Shamir, Ruby. *What's the Big Deal About First Ladies?* New York, NY: Philomel Books, 2017.

WEBSITES

First Ladies Research
www.firstladies.org/biographies
Learn all about the other First Ladies!

Melania Trump: First Lady of the United States
www.whitehouse.gov/people/melania-trump/
Read Melania's official White House biography.

INDEX